THE FAMILY BUSINESS

Breaking the Cycles That Bind Generations

Tonia Leslie

Scripture quotations unless otherwise noted, Scripture quotations are from the English Standard Version® (ESV®), copyright © 2001 by Crossway, a publishing ministry of Good News Publishers. Used by permission. All rights reserved.

Scripture quotations marked KJV are from the King James Version of the Bible, which is in the public domain.

The Family Business: Breaking the Cycles That Bind Generations

ISBN: 979-8-9995410-0-0

Printed in the United States of America

First Edition

Published by Tonia Leslie

Atlanta, Georgia

Disclaimer

The information provided is for educational and inspirational purposes. While the author has made every effort to provide accurate information, the author and publisher assume no responsibility for errors, omissions, or contrary interpretations of the subject matter.

This book is not intended as a substitute for professional counseling, therapy, or medical advice. Readers should consult appropriate professionals for specific guidance related to their individual circumstances.

Table of Contents

Foreword

G rowing up, I heard the same conversations echoing through our house: "We don't have money for that." "Money doesn't grow on trees." "We can't afford it." My family always managed to pay the bills on time. Still, financial stress was our constant companion, and money was always presented as something scarce, something to worry about rather than something to master.

For generations, the women in my family had accepted this relationship with money. They worked hard and did their best with what they had, but financial stability always seemed just out of reach. Money wasn't something we discussed openly, and the idea of financial freedom was unimaginable.

But something inside me refused to accept that this was as good as it gets.

When I told my grandmother that I was going to college to become a computer engineer (a teacher had said to me that I could make a lot of money in this profession), she was my biggest cheerleader. My grandmother had always believed that education was the pathway to a better life. "Go to school," she would say. "That's how you get ahead." I was determined not to live paycheck to paycheck, not to stress over every unexpected expense. I wanted to be debt-free, financially stable, and free to travel the world.

This book changed my perspective on family inheritance and the power we have to transform generational patterns. When I read these pages, I saw my own journey reflected, the decision to break free from "the family business" of financial struggle and create something different for future generations.

Tonia's courage in sharing her family's story gave me the language to express my own experience. Her discovery that good intentions alone aren't enough to break generational cycles resonated deeply. This book helped me realize that my pursuit of financial education wasn't just about me; it was about every woman in my family line who had dreamed of financial freedom but didn't know how to achieve it.

Today, financial stress is no longer "the family business." Through deliberate planning and applying wealth-building principles, my family's narrative has changed. My child is growing up with a different soundtrack, one that speaks of financial possibilities and the belief that they can achieve both security and their dreams.

This book will challenge you to examine the stories running through your own family line. You have the power to choose differently, to break cycles, and to become the ancestor your future generations will thank. The family business doesn't have to remain the same.

Our story is still being written. Let's make it count!

Sharnecia Williams
Family Pattern Breaker

Introduction

Every family has a story. Some families tell tales of triumph, legacy, and blessing passed down through generations. Others carry stories of pain, dysfunction, and destructive patterns that seem impossible to break. But here's what most people don't realize: you were not simply born into a family, you were born into a story that began long before you arrived, and that story will continue long after you leave.

The blood that flows through our veins tells a story. Often enough, people can look through their family history and determine, to a great extent, the course of their lives. Athletes often produce athletes, and musicians produce musicians. Families that have produced educators have a proud tradition of educators raising educators. Other families have many males who served in the armed forces, and oftentimes, the younger males find their identity in the same type of sacrifice to their country. Those positive traditions of strength, courage, community, and giving are often our focus as we strive to provide our children with direction for their future. When we see them struggling or unsure of their direction in life, we can easily suggest fields of service that are in their bloodline, because it's definitely in them.

Our blood heritage runs deeper than we often realize. The blood that flows through your veins is much older than you. It is actually the combination of all the people who make up your lineage. You may not have any knowledge of them, but their blood is the source of your very identity. Your ancestors are the blood that flows through you, and your bloodline makes you who you are in every aspect of your being. Knowingly or not, you are a combination of the mothers and fathers that existed before you, physically, mentally, emotionally, financially, and spiritually. This explains why you often lack answers to many of your actions, the situations you've encountered, and the relationships that have either formed or failed to develop.

It's like having a professional portrait taken. The photographer carefully selects a backdrop that will enhance the final image. Even though the background seems separate from you, it becomes integral to how the finished portrait looks. However, unlike a photographer's carefully chosen backdrop, our family background doesn't always create the perfect picture we envision for our lives.

Unlike a professional photographer who deliberately chooses complementary elements, we don't get to select our family backdrop. Yet this background—our ancestral history—profoundly shapes our life's portrait. We believe we created the picture of our lives; that it's authentically ours. We think our family history is far removed from us, with little significance in the picture of our lives.

But here's the truth: our ancestors often play a bigger part in the life portrait we have completed and what we still need to finish. They are even speaking louder and giving directions on how the picture will ultimately look. More than we realize, the patterns established by our ancestors influence decisions we believe are entirely our own. Through their blood that runs through our veins, they speak through us and for us, and this has helped form the picture of our lives.

This book will help you understand the story you've inherited, recognize the patterns that may be shaping your life, and most importantly, discover how to rewrite the narrative for yourself and future generations. While you can't change where you come from, you absolutely can change where your family is going. The question isn't whether your bloodline speaks, it's whether you're listening, and what you're going to do about what you hear.

CHAPTER 1

Now, Who Begot Whom Again

I f you're like most Christians, you've probably skipped over those long biblical genealogies filled with unpronounceable names. I certainly did. I was too eager to move along to the good stuff—King David, Joseph, Moses in Egypt, Daniel in the lions' den, and this list can go on and on. But I came to realize that the chapters of genealogies are just as important as the next chapter. Because through their bloodline, they were connected, and that bloodline helped to determine their very course in life.

These biblical genealogies aren't just ancient history—they reveal a spiritual principle that modern science now confirms. "But flesh with the life thereof, which is the blood thereof" (Genesis 9:4 KJV) and "For the life of the flesh is in the blood" (Leviticus 17:11 KJV). This is scientifically accurate. Half the DNA (genetic instructions) from the mother and half from the father contain all the information needed to create life. All of the genetic information (genes) we have comes from both parents, as well as both sets of grandparents, great-grandparents, and so on. The very blood in our bodies belongs to our ancestors, and who we are is the combination of their traits. Many of our issues stem from our gene pool.

God himself acknowledges this reality when He speaks of "visiting the iniquity of the fathers upon the children unto the third and fourth generation of them that hate me" (Exodus 20:5 KJV).

Many Christians struggle with persistent questions. Despite loving God, accepting Jesus as Lord and Savior, and faithfully praying, fasting, reading the Bible, and attending church, we still face problems we can't explain. These experiences leave us wondering if we truly understand the promises of God or the Bible that we read. Perhaps our answers lie in those genealogical chapters we skim over due to the difficulty of pronouncing names and a lack of understanding of their relevance in tracing these family lines. But there is relevancy in who begot you.

In the book of Genesis, God made a covenant with the blood of Abraham, Isaac, Jacob, and their descendants. This covenant reveals an important truth: the bloodline matters to God. Consider Solomon's story as evidence.

When Solomon disobeyed the Lord's commandment by pursuing other gods, God's response was telling. He said to Solomon, "... I will surely tear the kingdom from you ... Yet for the sake of David your father I will not do it in your days, but I will tear it out of the hand of your son." (1 Kings 11:11-12). Solomon's bloodline connection to David saved his throne.

This principle extends beyond biblical kings. Who has begotten you has a significant influence on your life, for good or for evil. Your physical traits, mental tendencies, financial patterns, natural abilities, and sometimes even spiritual inclinations come from those who have passed before you. The challenge is that we're often unaware of these inherited patterns, especially when we're unfamiliar with our family's past.

The biblical record shows us clear examples of inherited traits. Solomon inherited his father David's appetite for women. When the palace officials wanted to test whether David was truly dying, they placed two beautiful young women beside him in his bed, knowing his nature wouldn't allow him to resist. Solomon's appetite proved even greater than his father's.

Consider Jacob, who mastered deception with his mother's help. Where did this skill come from? His fathers! Abraham and Isaac were both deceptive when they claimed their wives were their sisters to protect themselves from harm. The pattern of barrenness among wives also repeated through generations, starting with Abraham. Just as the sons of Abraham inherited their father's business, daughters inherit their mother's business, because of the blood.

Your bloodline testifies loud and clear, but in most cases, we are not listening with our eyes. We fail to observe the repeated negative patterns in our lives that echo our ancestors' struggles. Yet the truth remains: if our ancestors did good things, our bloodline testifies to those good things. If they committed wickedness or evil, our blood testifies to those things as well.

The blood gives life to the dust from which we are made, and whatever affects the body, the blood remembers. That which we do repeatedly becomes encoded in our DNA, whether good or bad, right or wrong. The blood speaks, the blood cries, and it influences the experiences that come into our world according to what our genetic code declares.

Scripture confirms this reality throughout history. In the book of Exodus, the blood applied to the doorposts spoke to the angel of death, causing him to pass by and protecting those inside. When Cain killed Abel, God said him, "⸢What hast thou done? the voice of thy brother's blood crieth unto me from the ground" (Genesis 4:10 KJV).

This spiritual inheritance traces back to the beginning. In Genesis chapter 3, Adam's single act of disobedience led God to pronounce a curse between the seed of the woman and the seed of the serpent.

This act planted the seed of rebellion in humanity's blood, affecting every subsequent generation. Every person born of a woman inherits the consequences of sin through their bloodline, except Jesus.

The Apostle Paul describes this inherited condition in Ephesians 2:2-3: "following the course of this world, following the prince of the power of the air, the spirit that is now at work in the sons of disobedience... among whom we all once lived in the passions of our flesh." Before Christ, we were spiritually dead, driven by fleshly desires and enslaved to patterns of disobedience that controlled our minds, bodies, and spirits.

However, according to Hebrews 12:24, the blood of Jesus speaks better things than the blood of Abel. While our ancestral blood may cry out with pain, sin, and dysfunction, Christ's blood speaks of redemption, healing, and transformation over our family lines.

Here's the hope: understanding this inheritance is the first step toward freedom. When you recognize both the destructive patterns and the divine calling in your bloodline, you can begin to break free from generational bondage and embrace the life God intended for your family.

CHAPTER 2

The Call That Broke the Silence

Mom, this pattern stops with me—it goes no further," I yelled into the phone, my voice shaking with the weight of what I'd just learned. I was standing outside the hair salon on a warm, sunny day, but even now, I still can't remember what led up to that life-changing conversation.

I was thirty-three years old when my mother told me that she was not married to my father when she had my brothers. Finding that out at my age was shocking, not because my parents weren't married (is anyone even considered illegitimate anymore?), but because she had never mentioned it before. "You are just now telling me this!" "You don't think this is something you should've said before now?" And I kept yelling at her in disbelief and anger... "Don't you know that if you had just talked to us, told us this earlier, we probably would not have had children before marriage?"

My mother's reply cut through my accusations: "It's my business, I don't have to tell anyone my business." I hated hearing her response, but I wasn't surprised by it. She was from another time, where people buried their painful experiences rather than discuss them. Each trauma was buried beneath the next, creating a foundation of silence and secrets. Nothing was ever addressed or spoken about. You just kept surviving, kept protecting yourself, and kept hiding the painful truths.

Once you decide to have children, you pass on more than just your physical traits, your smile, your walk, your mannerisms. You also pass on your patterns, your choices, and your unspoken struggles. What was once your private pain becomes the family legacy. My mother now had four daughters, and her three oldest had each followed the same pattern: children born outside of marriage with different fathers. What she thought was her personal business had become our inherited blueprint, a generational cycle that seemed to put each daughter under its influence. Standing there, shaking my head in disbelief, I was determined that this pattern would stop with me.

There's a haunting truth from The Color Purple that resonates with many women: "A girl child ain't safe in a family of men." This reality remains painfully accurate for many women today—mentally, emotionally, and physically unsafe in families where dysfunction runs deep. Often enough, the pain of our mothers and grandmothers came at the hands of the men in their lives—the ones they were given through blood and the ones they chose to give themselves to. The ones they chose often mirrored the negative patterns of the ones from their bloodline. Many of us find ourselves trapped in these cycles unknowingly, recreating the same painful dynamics of our mothers' lives.

My mother's life reflected the struggles of many women born in the South during that era. Born in North Carolina in 1939, she grew up at the end of the Great Depression when sharecropping—working someone else's land for a share of the crops—kept families in grinding poverty. She was the youngest of eight children. When her father died, she was nine and her mother died when she was thirteen, her world became even more unstable. Her oldest sister became her caretaker, and they lived in what she described as a house made of cardboard, speaking to the desperate poverty of their living conditions.

My mother had endured a hard life, though she carried herself with dignity. She would often joke that she had earned her doctorate degree from the school of "Hard Knocks." Her voice was quite proper as she explained that the University of Life had taught her well. I share my mother's history not to shame her—I truly love her dearly—but because I love my daughter more, and even more so, the daughters who are still to come. This legacy of repeated patterns that had entrapped the women of our family for years could be overcome by gaining knowledge and understanding of the past, thereby shifting our lives forward.

Sadly, I knew very little about her past. She didn't talk to me much about her life, like most mothers from that era whose teaching philosophy was "Do what I say because I say so." We were never given knowledge or understanding, so we lacked the wisdom needed to make better decisions or take a different path in life. The little I discovered about her past became invaluable in understanding the patterns of my own life, thanks to my brother and younger sister sharing what they knew.

When I moved to Georgia at eighteen for college and later started my own family, I missed the crucial years when our relationship should have transitioned from mother-daughter to mother-friend. We remained locked in the traditional mother-daughter dynamic throughout my adult years. So years later, after her death, I was left wondering about her life and how her relationships had affected her and, in essence, me. That's when my brother made his startling observation: "You married someone just like your daddy."

That was hard to grasp since I had rarely been around my biological father growing up and barely saw him as an adult. Since my mother was no longer available, I turned to the one person I knew would know her intimately: my youngest sister. I had always envied their friendship, watching their interactions during my visits, knowing that's how an adult relationship with your mother should be.

However, distance and circumstances had prevented that from happening for me.

When my mother and I should have been developing a friendship, sharing stories of past relationships and secrets that friends share, I was away in Georgia, raising a family. At that time, I had no interest in her history. My sister admitted that even she knew little—my mother was intensely private about her life. But the little my sister shared proved invaluable to my understanding.

My mother was a strong woman, but life's cruelties also hardened her, as many women become who endure repeated trauma. They don't choose to become what circumstances force them to become. They become what we might call soldiers—not by choice, but by necessity. Most women don't desire to be on the frontlines of any battle, but repeated, toxic, hurtful relationships eventually forge them into skillful life warriors. Unknowingly, they become permanently enlisted in survival mode. This was definitely true for my mother.

At sixteen, she experienced a trauma that would shape the rest of her life—she was assaulted by her older sister's friend. When she discovered she was pregnant, she had to leave school, abandoning her dreams of education. She often spoke of how much she loved learning and had been an excellent student before this violation stole her future. Her first child, born from this trauma, was a daughter.

During the birth of her second child, the father abandoned her while she was in labor. Now, a single mother of two daughters with no formal education or job training, she worked nights as a custodian to provide for her family. Tragically, she experienced another assault from a coworker during this vulnerable time.

Years later, while attending night school to finally earn her high school diploma, a dream deferred but not destroyed, she met my father. He was thirteen years older and lived in an upstairs apartment with his son. During their courtship, my two older brothers were born. As we became adults, my father made it painfully clear that he had never loved her but married her only because of her insistence that "I can't keep having babies like this."

During that time in Virginia, my brothers wouldn't have been considered his legal sons since my parents weren't married when they were born. Can you imagine finally pursuing your education after years of struggle, only to fall for a man who didn't love you and find yourself pregnant again? The home environment was tumultuous, according to my brother. My father was abusive, and many nights my mother slept on the sofa in my brothers' room for safety.

She was surprised to discover she was pregnant with me because intimacy between my parents had become rare—he was involved with other women. During one of his phone calls with another woman, my mother listened in on the extension. When he discovered her eavesdropping, his rage was terrifying. I was two years old, and my brothers were six and seven when the violence escalated beyond anything they had witnessed before.

My brothers still remember that day in vivid detail. My father tried to strike my mother over the head with a large wooden chair, but she raised her arm defensively, and he broke it instead. As she clutched her injured arm, trying to escape, my eleven-year-old sister struck him in the head with a hammer, giving my mother a chance to flee. My sister ran behind her while my father shot at them as they escaped. She was just an eleven-year-old girl, bearing the weight of protecting her mother.

9

There are two images burned into my memory from that day: my oldest brother standing frozen in the kitchen where it all happened, and the sound of men working outside—a normal day continuing while our world fell apart. No one stopped to help as my father's violence shattered our family.

Years later, as I reflected on my mother's journey, I began to understand how her unspoken trauma had shaped not just her life, but mine as well. Despite all the pain and struggle, she had also received blessings along the way, and both the wounds and the gifts would become part of our family's inheritance.

Our legacy of pain would echo through generations until someone chose to break the silence and tell a different story.

CHAPTER 3

What Runs in the Family

J ust as my mother's patterns were passed down to the next generation, nature itself demonstrates how traits and behaviors are inherited through generations. Animals are not taught how to behave like animals; this behavior is inherent to their species. Each animal has their own language and characteristics that distinguish them from other species. The nuances of the species are encoded in the blood of each animal and passed down with each birth.

Groundbreaking neuroscientific research on mice has proven that trauma can be inherited. Scientists trained mice to fear a specific smell, and remarkably, their descendants were born with the same fear, even though they had never encountered the smell or been trained to fear it. It is theorized that certain memories from parents can be inherited and encoded in the child's DNA at birth. This research confirms that subsequent generations are affected by the experiences of their parents.

Disney's film *Secretariat* tells a powerful story about the importance of bloodlines. In this movie, a wife and mother must take over her parents' horse farm after her mother dies and her father becomes too ill to run it. The story illustrates how understanding one's bloodline can lead to extraordinary success.

After her mother's death, she discovered a coin toss agreement her father had made with the wealthiest man in America at that time. This coin toss would determine who got the first pick of foals born from her father's two mares and the rich man's stallion. Although she lost the coin toss, she still got what she wanted when choosing a horse. She based her selection on something more valuable than luck, knowledge of bloodlines.

There are studbooks for horses that provide official records of pedigree, tracking the parents and genetic heritage of each animal. Through careful study of these bloodline records, she discovered that while the stallion was fast, he lacked stamina over long distances. Her father's two mares presented an interesting choice: the younger mare was ideal for breeding because horses tend to produce better racehorses in their prime years. However, the older mare had a grandfather with exceptional stamina, a crucial trait for distance racing.

Armed with this bloodline knowledge, she made an informed decision that led to Secretariat, a horse that not only won the Triple Crown but set racing records that have never been matched. She gambled wisely because she understood the genetic heritage she was working with.

The same principle that guided her success with Secretariat also applies to human families. Just as she studied horse pedigrees to predict outcomes, we can observe traits passed down through human bloodlines. The Apostle Paul understood this when he wrote to Timothy, " I am reminded of your sincere faith, a faith that dwelt first in your grandmother Lois and your mother Eunice and now, I am sure, dwells in you as well. For this reason I remind you to fan into flame the gift of God, which is in you through the laying on of my hands" (2 Timothy 1:5-6), just as physical traits and abilities are passed down through bloodlines, spiritual qualities like faith can also be inherited and strengthened across generations.

In the world of sports, we consistently see how exceptional abilities are often passed down through family lines. LeBron James, a basketball legend, is now watching his sons, Bronny and Bryce, follow in his footsteps on the court. Deion Sanders, nicknamed "Prime Time," dominated both football and baseball and was inducted into the Pro Football Hall of Fame. Now, his sons, Shilo and Shedeur, are standing on his shoulders, continuing the family legacy in football.

The Manning family represents a true football dynasty. Beginning with Archie Manning, who played at both the collegiate and professional levels, the genetic gift for quarterbacking was passed on to his sons, Peyton and Eli, both of whom had outstanding collegiate and NFL careers. Now we see the next generation emerging with Arch Manning, who appears to be following the same prolific path as his uncles.

In golf, Charlie Woods is developing into an excellent player, following in the footsteps of his father, Tiger, a trajectory that we could have predicted based on his bloodline.

The pattern continues across all areas of talent and ability. Music provides an equally compelling example. Mariah Carey's voice is regarded as one of the most iconic and versatile in music history. Still, this gift can be traced back to her mother, Patricia Carey, a Juilliard-trained opera singer and vocal coach. The vocal ability that made Mariah famous was already present in her genetic heritage.

While these examples showcase the positive side of genetic inheritance, the same principle applies to less desirable traits and patterns as well. Many of us may not have inspiring bloodlines like those mentioned, but we still follow patterns established by our parents.

I experienced this firsthand when I realized I had repeated my mother's relationship patterns without even knowing it. Even though my parents divorced when I was young and my father wasn't a significant part of my life, I still ended up recreating an almost exact replica of my mother's marriage experience. Just as my mother had my two oldest brothers with my father before they were married, I too was pregnant when I got married. I thought my husband loved me because I had told him, 'Do not marry me if you don't love me', words that echoed my mother's plea to my father decades earlier.

When my mother and older sister would tell me stories about my father and their relationship, I began to see similar character traits in my husband. How did those same undesirable conditions repeat in my life? Unfortunately, because I didn't know enough about my father and my parents' marriage, the same cycle of hurt and disappointment happened in my generation.

The cycles keep repeating when you don't know the truth. How can you walk in wisdom when there is no understanding? How can you expect your children to have a better path in life if they are not given the knowledge and understanding needed to choose differently? No matter how painful the truth may be to face, understanding can break negative cycles when wisdom is applied to our lives. Your willingness to confront family patterns determines whether the next generation will repeat them or break free from them. By not discussing your history or your family's patterns, you prevent the next generation from moving forward.

God said, "My people are destroyed for lack of knowledge" (Hosea 4:6 KJV). Because there was no understanding, the devastation of broken homes and unhealthy relationships continued into another generation. I am not saying that all issues can be prevented, but better decisions can be made when we are given the tools of knowledge—the who, what, when, where, why, and how. Knowledge of the truth and understanding of the past will help the next generation apply wisdom in their lives.

Whether positive or negative, the traits flowing through your bloodline are real and powerful. The question is: which patterns will you choose to nurture, and which will you choose to break? Understanding your genetic heritage, both the gifts and the challenges, is essential for making informed decisions about your family's future.

CHAPTER 4

The Daughter I Wanted to Save

There's a Christmas movie that perfectly captures what every parent wishes they could give their children. *Throwback Holiday* tells the story of a woman who gets a second chance at her high school years, armed with the wisdom she has gained as an adult. In this story, she makes better choices the second time around because she knows how everything will turn out. It's a lot easier to make the right decisions when you already have all the answers. Hindsight is definitely twenty-twenty. At the end of the movie, after she has received everything she wanted—a great career, a loving husband, three beautiful children, and her mother (who had died in her original timeline), she offers a prayer of thanksgiving: "God, thank you for showing me that I made all the right choices along the way to end up exactly where I'm supposed to be."

Watching her make "all the right choices" with future knowledge made me realize what I wanted for my own daughter, the impossible gift of perfect foresight to avoid all the mistakes I had made. How can anyone make all the right choices in life? It's impossible, but that's what I desperately wanted for my daughter.

Every Christmas, when we should have been focusing on trucks and action figures for my three sons, I would slip away and wander down the aisles of baby dolls, play kitchens, and dollhouses, longing for a daughter. I would get lost in that precious time and space, imagining what Christmas would look like if I had a girl. However, I would be interrupted by my husband's voice saying, "And what are you doing here?" before being pulled back into the reality that the toys were for the boys.

While I was pregnant with my fourth child, God told me that He was giving me a girl. I was so grateful to have her. She was born two years after my third son, and the house would never be the same again.

As a young girl, her oldest brother would often tell her, "If you had never come into the family, it would've been boring. You bring the spice to the house." He described their conversations as being on a rollercoaster ride. With three older brothers and one younger, she was well protected and became the second mother of the house. She was outspoken and outgoing, but she was also her brothers' fierce advocate, promptly speaking up for anyone she felt needed help. She was involved in ballet and tap, and of course, she was a softball slugger. She was the epitome of the princess of the house. I enjoyed watching her grow up and develop into a young woman, so my hopes for her future were quite high. She aimed for and achieved more than I had ever expected.

Then came the phone call with my mother that changed everything. While talking to her that day outside the hair salon, all I could see was my daughter's future; she could not end up like me. Her life was too promising, her potential too great. And I declared with fierce determination, "This stops with me; it goes no farther. We will not keep having babies like this."

From that moment forward, I became intentional about breaking the cycle. When my daughter was a teenager, we spent many car rides to the mall discussing the realities of sex, relationships, and consequences. I shared the mistakes I had made at a young age and all the things that romantic movies, TV shows, and books never address. I was open and transparent about my teenage life and my relationship with her father. I thought I was giving her the wisdom I never had.

Years later, I thought I had succeeded in breaking the cycle. My daughter remained a virgin until marriage, so surely, I had won. But life had other lessons to teach me about the complexity of generational patterns.

It wasn't until my daughter was pursuing her master's degree in psychology that we both discovered how much I had missed. A genomics assignment required her to research both parents' family histories, and what we found was sobering.

The assignment revealed striking similarities between our family lines. Both sides can be traced back to Native American and African ancestry. Both sets of grandparents had been sharecroppers, struggling with poverty. Both families had produced business owners and other positive examples.

However, the darker patterns were equally prominent: broken marriages were equally prevalent on both sides, with few remaining married and many staying single. Children born to multiple partners outside of marriage were a common thread. Most concerning of all, abuse—physical, emotional, and mental—had affected the women at the hands of men on both sides of the bloodline.

I was so focused on preventing one specific outcome for my daughter, having children outside of marriage, that I had missed the deeper, more complex web of inherited behaviors and relationship patterns.

Children born outside of marriage should not have been my only concern. If I had understood the other patterns running through both bloodlines, the cycles of broken relationships, the tendency toward abuse, the repeated emotional trauma, I could have prepared her for challenges I never saw coming. My narrow focus had left her vulnerable to generational issues I had never even been aware of.

When the genomics assignment revealed the full scope of our family inheritance, I realized that love and good intentions weren't enough. Breaking generational cycles requires more than addressing the obvious problems; it demands understanding the complete picture of what runs in your family line.

CHAPTER 5

Understanding Brings Change

The genomics assignment my daughter completed revealed how much I had missed about our family patterns. But this challenge of incomplete family knowledge isn't new. Throughout history, understanding family dynamics has been crucial for preventing repeated mistakes and making informed decisions about the future.

Consider what happens when you visit a doctor for a comprehensive health evaluation. Beyond examining your current condition, they always ask about your family's medical history. Will knowing your family's medical history help prevent what might otherwise be inevitable? This is a resounding yes! Often, doctors will suggest specific tests to determine your risk level for inherited medical conditions and recommend preventive measures to stop those conditions from developing.[1] We can apply this type of preventive approach to other areas of family history.

However, if we don't know our family history, it becomes impossible to stop the repetition of destructive patterns. I have a friend who illustrates this challenge perfectly. Despite her faithful Christian Walk and devoted spiritual practices, she faces constant setbacks and struggles. Nothing works in her favor, no matter how hard she tries or how much she prays. What makes her situation particularly challenging is that she was adopted as a baby and has no access to her family's patterns—medical, emotional, relational, or spiritual. She cannot apply preventive wisdom because she doesn't know what she's preventing. Her unknown bloodline speaks, but she cannot hear or respond to its testimony. Without this crucial information, she navigates life without the benefit of understanding her genetic and spiritual heritage.

The principle of knowledge preventing problems isn't limited to modern times. Throughout scripture, we see how understanding family patterns could have prevented significant pain and dysfunction. Genesis 37 begins the account of Joseph's trials, which started with family dynamics that could have been managed differently. His brothers despised him after their father Jacob showed blatant favoritism by making him a coat of many colors. When Joseph shared dreams that suggested he would rule over his family, their jealousy reached a breaking point. By verse 20, Joseph's brothers devised a plan to kill him, saying, "Come now therefore, and let us slay him, and cast him into some pit, and we will say, some evil beast hath devoured him: and we shall see what become of his dreams."

Their scheme involved taking Joseph's coat, killing a goat, and dipping the coat in blood to deceive their father. When they presented the bloodied coat to Jacob, he believed their deception and concluded that "a fierce animal has devoured him. Joseph is without doubt torn to pieces." (Genesis 37:33). This was the same Jacob who had deceived his own father, Isaac, by using Esau's clothes to steal his blessing. The pattern of deception that Jacob had used against his brother continued with his sons. Could this crisis have been prevented if Jacob had recognized his own tendency toward favoritism and deception? What if he had spoken to Joseph about keeping his dreams private? Perhaps the family trauma could have been avoided entirely.

Moses provides another compelling example. Numbers 12:3 describes him as the humblest man on earth at that time—he was patient and lowly, possessing the exact qualities needed to lead the stiff-necked and rebellious Israelites. He often repented on their behalf to spare them from God's punishment. Yet in Numbers 20, when the Israelites complained about a lack of water, Moses' response was telling. God instructed him to speak to the rock to bring forth water, but Moses, apparently angry and frustrated, said to the people, "Hear now, you rebels: shall we bring water for you out of this rock?" Then he struck the rock twice. This single act of anger cost him the privilege of leading the Israelites into the Promised Land.

Here's what makes this significant: Moses was from the tribe of Levi. In Genesis 49, Jacob specifically cursed the anger of Levi and Simeon, calling them "weapons of violence." Levi and Simeon had killed an entire village of men in Genesis 34 because the prince of the city had dishonored their sister Dinah. Their anger led them to take revenge on innocent people. How would Moses have known about this inherited tendency toward destructive anger? He grew up in Pharaoh's house, separated from his own family's history. If he had been aware of this pattern in his lineage, could he have exercised better self-control? Might he have been better prepared to manage the anger that ultimately prevented him from entering the Promised Land?

Understanding your family history provides a roadmap for both opportunities and challenges. I've seen this principle work in both directions throughout my life. I have a friend whose younger sister is an exceptionally talented baker. Over the years, she has felt that her mother was meant to have had a baking business. Her sister possesses the same remarkable gift, but neither pursued baking commercially. Even though the family gift is obvious, no one has started this particular "family business," despite the clear calling and ability.

On the positive side, another friend made an early decision to achieve financial stability and took deliberate steps to make it happen. Her motivation came directly from her family experience—as a child, she constantly heard that money didn't grow on trees, and we don't have money for that. She chose to study computer information systems because a teacher told her that she could make "good money" in technology. Later, she followed the advice of wealth advisors and successful businesspeople, educating herself in wealth management and putting those principles into practice. Through her intentional choices, poverty is no longer "the family business."

I've also met a woman who was afraid to marry, despite having numerous successful long-term relationships. As we talked throughout the day, I learned about her childhood and her mother's experiences. Her mother was a beautiful southern woman who attracted many suitors but repeatedly married men who became physically abusive. Additionally, this woman was molested by one of her mother's male friends during childhood. Because of this family trauma, she had made a conscious vow never to marry, determined not to repeat the cycle of abuse she had witnessed and experienced.

These examples illustrate how family patterns—both positive and negative—get passed down through generations, sometimes in ways we don't fully understand. Pastor Myles Munroe taught a powerful principle that explains this phenomenon: "In you are nations." This means everything—good or bad, right or wrong, you do with your body, you are also doing to your seed. If you engage in extramarital relationships, have multiple sexual partners, or consume excessive amounts of alcohol or drugs, your seed carries the memory of these experiences because your blood remembers. It becomes part of your genetic and spiritual memory.

This principle has biblical foundations that go back to the very beginning of humanity. God created mankind in Adam, and in Adam, all humans existed. Because Adam sinned, all humans who enter the earth receive the consequences of his actions, which demonstrates how one person's choices can affect entire generations.

We also see this principle at work in the story of Abraham. God told him, " I will make of you a great nation, and I will bless you and make your name great, so that you will be a blessing" (Genesis 12:2). True to His promise, God later changed Abram's name to Abraham because his seed would carry nations within (Genesis 17:4-5). Not only did God bless Isaac, the child of promise, but He also blessed Abraham's other son, Ishmael, because he, too, was part of Abraham's bloodline.

The concept of carrying "nations within" becomes even clearer in the story of Rebecca. In Genesis 25:22-23, when she was pregnant with twins who "struggled together within her," God told her, "Two nations are in thy womb, and two manner of people shall be separated from thy bowels." In this scripture, it reveals that women are carriers of seed and destiny—even though women don't technically have seed in the biological sense, they are the vessels who bring life and legacy into the world through their wombs.

We are called to live lives that cause others to thrive. Just as trees and plants give life to their environment, we are meant to give life to those around us and those who come after us. But how can we give life in areas that are spiritually dead or cursed? Can future generations thrive when they inherit patterns of dysfunction and death?

Consider Abraham's father, Terah, who took his family toward Canaan but stopped at Haran and settled there permanently (Genesis 11:31). After Terah's death, God told Abraham to leave that country and go to the land He would show him—Canaan, the very destination his father had abandoned. Psalm 33:11 tells us that " The counsel of the LORD stands forever, the plans of his heart to all generations." What God has planned for your family remains with the family until someone fulfills it.

Understanding your family history, both the struggles and the strengths, gives you the power to make informed decisions about your future. Knowledge doesn't guarantee a perfect path, but it provides the wisdom to navigate more skillfully and prepare the next generation for what lies ahead. When you recognize the patterns that have held your family back and the gifts that have been underutilized, you can make conscious choices to break destructive cycles and activate dormant blessings. You become the generation that changes the family's trajectory.

CHAPTER 6

Tell the Story That Must Be Told

After understanding how family patterns get passed down through generations, the question becomes: how do we ensure the next generation learns from our discoveries? The answer lies in an old tradition that holds powerful lessons for modern families.

Consider the intricate patterns of a handmade quilt. In earlier generations, these weren't just blankets; they were family stories sewn in fabric. Older women would create quilts using pieces of old clothing from loved ones, incorporating memories of people, events, and family culture into the design. A patch from grandfather's work shirt, a piece of grandmother's wedding dress, and fabric from a baby's first outfit, each piece told part of the family's story. Often, a family's entire history could be traced through the patterns of a single quilt.

Just as those quilters preserved family history through fabric, someone in every generation must become the family storyteller. Someone has to notice the patterns, both positive and negative, and decide to share what they mean for future generations. If alcoholism runs in the family line, you may choose not to drink and openly discuss why, allowing the next generation to see a different path. If family history shows a pattern of stopping education at high school, someone can pursue higher learning and explain the importance of breaking that limitation. Someone must be willing to identify destructive patterns and courageously change the family narrative.

But there's a problem that runs deep in many families: silence. The more painful an experience, the deeper it gets buried. Each trauma layer is beneath the next, creating foundations built on secrets rather than truth. This silence comes at a tremendous cost, as Maya Angelou observed: "There is no greater agony than bearing an untold story inside you."[2]

You would be surprised by the untold dreams and hopes buried in our mothers' hearts. But why would they discuss aspirations that seemed impossible to achieve? They had to work, raise families, and survive within the constraints of their time and circumstances. Many couldn't pursue the dreams that lived in their hearts, so those dreams remained unspoken, undiscovered by their children.

In the 1980s, many young women were encouraged to attend college precisely because their mothers hadn't had the same opportunities. These mothers had entered the workplace without formal education and observed that people with degrees fared better. They encouraged, sometimes insisted, that their daughters pursue higher education, even when they couldn't fully articulate their own, often unspoken, dreams of learning and achievement.

I discovered this reality in my own family through baking. In high school, I took home economics and fell in love with creating cakes and cookies. I became the designated baker for our holiday meals and continued baking for my own family years later. One evening, a prophet told me I came from a line of bakers, something I had never known. When I called my mother the next day to share this revelation, she confirmed it: "We had some great bakers in the family." Yet she had never mentioned this heritage before. Years after her death, my sister revealed that our mother had always wanted to own a restaurant and had envisioned all her children helping to run it. This was one of her unfulfilled dreams.

Many people exhibit this pattern of inherited gifts and dreams if you pay close attention. I know hairstylists in Georgia and Virginia whose stories illustrate this beautifully. The stylist in Georgia never wanted a corporate job; she loved beauty and pursued her gift for hair and nails. Her daughter, despite declaring as a child that she would never be a stylist, eventually followed the same path and expanded into makeup artistry. The Virginia stylist wanted to attend beauty school, but her mother discouraged her because other family members had training they never used. So, she earned a four-year degree in marketing, handed it to her mother upon graduation, and then attended beauty school anyway. Today, she and her daughter run a salon together, with the daughter having also earned a college degree before embracing the family gift.

These stories point to a profound truth: the dreams we think are uniquely our own often belong to our family's legacy. Maya Angelou expressed this sentiment: "Bring the gifts that my ancestors gave. I am the hope and the dream of the slave."[3] Because previous generations were unable to fulfill specific dreams, God has given those desires to you. Psalm 37:4 promises, "he will give you the desires of your heart." Often, what we think are our personal dreams are actually the unfulfilled callings of those who came before us.

Modern science confirms what families have long observed: certain experiences, behaviors, and even trauma can be passed down through generations. Research on Holocaust survivors, studies of inherited resilience, and investigations into how historical trauma affects descendants provide compelling evidence for these generational patterns. The same biological mechanisms that can transmit challenges also have the power to pass down strength, creativity, and positive adaptations (see Appendix A for detailed research).

This understanding of generational inheritance isn't just a modern discovery; Scripture has long revealed the power of passing down both stories and callings through family lines. In 2 Samuel 7, David dreamed of building a temple for God, but it was his son Solomon who fulfilled that vision. The children of Israel knew that God would bring them to the Promised Land because the promise had been passed down through generations. Joseph commanded that his bones be taken out of Egypt because he knew God's promise to give Abraham's descendants their own land. When these stories were passed down faithfully, they became sources of hope and direction.

In Judges 6:13, when Gideon questioned God's presence during difficult times, he asked, "where are all his wonderful deeds that our fathers recounted to us?" Because previous generations had shared their stories of God's deliverance, Gideon could believe it was possible for his generation, too. The stories gave him hope and context for his calling.

There is a legacy waiting to be discovered when we understand the gifts, dreams, and hopes of our mothers and fathers. Would we be more motivated to pursue these dreams if we understood our ancestors shared them? Would we recognize them as callings from God for our family lineage? When we miss our true purpose by not living out these inherited dreams, we rob not only ourselves but also those who passed them down and those still to come.

But breaking generational patterns requires both understanding and action. I saw a powerful demonstration of this principle in a short video. A young man used four empty glasses to represent four generations: grandparents, parents, oneself, and one's child. He poured red liquid (representing a generational curse) from the first glass through the second and into the third, explaining that this represented you inheriting the family pattern. Then he said, "You must decide that this pattern stops with you." He poured clear water into the third glass while the red liquid was still there. As the water diluted the red, it gradually became clear. "Breaking generational patterns takes time and work," he explained, "but when you pour into the fourth glass, your child, the liquid runs clear. The next generation inherits freedom instead of bondage."

Someone in every generation must be willing to tell the story that needs to be told. Someone must break the silence, acknowledge both the pain and the promise, and give the next generation the gift of truth. You may be that person for your family. The question isn't whether your family has a story worth telling; every family does. The question is whether you'll be brave enough to tell it.

CHAPTER 7

The Blood Still Speaks

After understanding the importance of sharing family stories and breaking generational patterns, the question arises: what hope do we have for genuine transformation? The answer lies in a spiritual reality that changes everything about our inheritance.

We've seen how the blood of our ancestors speaks—sometimes declaring blessings, sometimes crying out with pain and dysfunction. We've learned that our bloodlines carry both gifts and burdens, patterns that can either propel us forward or hold us back. But here's the hope that changes everything: we don't have to remain prisoners of our ancestral inheritance.

According to Hebrews 12:24, the blood of Jesus speaks better things than that of Abel. Abel's blood cried out for justice after his murder, but Jesus' blood speaks of mercy, redemption, and transformation. While our ancestral blood may testify of generational curses, Christ's blood testifies of generational blessings. His blood doesn't just cover your sins, it covers your inheritance, speaking better things over your family's future.

The metaphor of grafting can help describe this transformation. In agriculture, grafting joins two plants into one by creating a wound in a strong, healthy tree and inserting a branch from another plant. As they heal together, the grafted branch draws life from the stronger root system, gaining access to better nutrients and greater vigor than it could ever have had on its own.

Spiritually, this is what happens when we accept Christ as our Lord and Savior: we are supernaturally grafted into God's family tree. Colossians 1:13 tells us that God "has delivered us from the domain of darkness and transferred us to the kingdom of his beloved Son." We become part of a different bloodline—one that speaks of victory instead of defeat, blessing instead of curse, hope instead of despair.

When you are grafted into Christ's bloodline, His blood begins to speak over your family line. If the blood of a lamb in Exodus could speak to the death angel and cause him to pass over, how much more can the blood of Jesus speak life and transformation over your generational patterns?

The beginning of this spiritual transformation starts with renewing your mind. Romans 12:2 tells us, "be transformed by the renewal of your mind, that by testing you may discern what is the will of God, what is good and acceptable and perfect." The patterns established by your ancestors don't have to continue controlling your thoughts, decisions, and actions. As God's truth renews your mind, you begin to think differently about your family's possibilities and align your thoughts with what Christ's blood is declaring over your inheritance.

Jesus said, "behold, the kingdom of God is within you" (Luke 17:21 KJV). This means that God's power to transform generational patterns isn't something distant, it's accessible right now, in your heart and mind. The key is learning to hear what Christ's blood is saying about your family, rather than only hearing what your ancestral blood has been declaring.

Once you understand what Christ's blood is declaring over your family line, you can begin to identify the specific blessings God has in store for you. Just as Jesus told the woman in Luke 13:16 that because she was "a daughter of Abraham," she should be "loosed from" her infirmities, you too have a spiritual inheritance that can override your natural one.

Consider the widow in 2 Kings 4, who was drowning in debt and on the verge of losing her sons. When she turned to God's prophet for help and followed his instructions, her family transitioned from a system of lack to one of abundance. When we become aware of destructive patterns plaguing our families, we can turn to God and receive answers from His system of blessing rather than remaining trapped in generational struggle.

The manifestation of this transformation also shows up throughout history in practical ways. Consider gospel artist Fred Hammond, whose mother couldn't afford the musical equipment he needed as a young man playing in church. She couldn't buy it outright, but she asked about a payment plan, believing in her son's gift. That investment of faith launched a career that enabled him to buy his mother a home and support his siblings through school. What had been "not having enough" in the family's history became abundance through one generation's decision to believe in God's calling.

Similarly, George Foreman's story demonstrates how God can use the very thing that seems wrong to bring a breakthrough. His family was trapped in severe poverty, and his mother initially opposed his boxing, thinking it was wrong. But God used the gift she questioned to deliver their entire family from lack. Sometimes what we think is unlikely or even inappropriate becomes the very thing God uses to transform our family's trajectory.

Both stories reveal a powerful truth: when we align our faith with God's plan for our bloodline, He can turn our greatest struggles into our greatest victories.

The beauty of spiritual grafting is that every bloodline problem must eventually give way to the benefits of being connected to Christ's bloodline. When you understand that you're not limited by your family's past but empowered by God's future, you begin to live differently. You make decisions based on where God is taking your family, not where it's been.

While the next generation will inherit certain natural tendencies and face specific family challenges, they also inherit the power to overcome through Christ's blood. The same bloodline that may carry struggles also carries the capacity for breakthrough, because it has been grafted into the source of all blessings.

Your family's story doesn't have to end with the patterns that brought pain. You can mark the beginning of a new chapter of breakthrough, blessing, and transformation. The blood still speaks—but now it speaks of victory, hope, and the unlimited possibilities that come from being grafted into God's family tree.

Appendix A:

The Science Behind Generational Inheritance

Modern science has begun to validate what families have observed for generations: certain experiences, behaviors, and even trauma can be passed down through bloodlines. This research provides compelling evidence for the principles discussed throughout this book.

A.1: Epigenetic Inheritance - How Experiences Shape DNA

Epigenetic inheritance explains how various factors and experiences can influence gene expression and be passed down from one generation to the next, thereby affecting traits and behaviors. Unlike genetic mutations, epigenetic changes don't alter the DNA sequence itself but rather affect how genes are expressed.

Scientists have discovered that trauma, stress, and even PTSD can leave molecular scars on our DNA that get passed to future generations. These changes can influence everything from stress response to immune system function, helping explain why certain patterns seem to "run in families" beyond simple environmental factors.

A.2: Holocaust Survivor Studies - Evidence of Inherited Trauma

Groundbreaking research conducted by Professor Rachel Yehuda at the Icahn School of Medicine at Mount Sinai Medical School in New York has provided compelling evidence that trauma can indeed be biologically inherited.[5]

Key Findings:

2020 Study Results: Yehuda's research team studied Holocaust survivors and their children, revealing that participants carried changes to genes linked to cortisol levels, which are involved in the body's stress response. These genetic changes were found in both the survivors and their offspring, even though the children had never experienced the original trauma.[4]

2021 Follow-up Study: Further research revealed changes in gene expression associated with immune system function. These changes weaken the barrier function of white blood cells, allowing the immune system to become involved in the central nervous system inappropriately. This interference has been linked to increased rates of depression, anxiety, psychosis, and autism spectrum disorders.[5]

Implications:

This research suggests that the effects of severe trauma don't end with the individual who experienced it. The biological impact can be transmitted to children and potentially grandchildren, affecting their mental health, stress response, and overall well-being.

A.3: Trauma and Slavery - Understanding Historical Impact

The concept of epigenetic inheritance offers a scientific framework for understanding how the trauma of slavery might continue to affect descendants today. The violence, displacement, family separation, and systematic oppression faced by enslaved individuals created profound biological and psychological impacts that research suggests can be transmitted across generations.

Historical Context:

The trauma experienced during slavery was not just individual but systematic and cultural, affecting entire communities across multiple generations. This collective trauma may have created lasting biological changes that continue to influence stress response, health outcomes, and family dynamics in African American communities.

Resilience Factors:

However, research also shows that positive adaptations and resilience can be inherited through the same mechanisms. The strength, creativity, and survival skills developed by enslaved communities also became part of the genetic and cultural inheritance passed down to future generations.

A.4: The Moynihan Report and Academic Response

The Original Report (1965):

Sociologist Daniel Patrick Moynihan, later a U.S. Senator, released "The Negro Family: The Case for National Action" while working in the Johnson Administration's Labor Department.[6] Drawing on sociologist E. Franklin Frazier's work, Moynihan traced problems he observed in African American families directly back to slavery.[7]

Moynihan's Claims:

- Slavery created a "fatherless matrifocal (mother-centered) pattern" in black families

- Men didn't learn proper providing and protecting roles

- These deficiencies were passed down through generations

- Family structure problems were the primary cause of ongoing difficulties

Academic Response - Herbert Gutman's Research:

The Counter-Study (1976): Historian Herbert Gutman undertook extensive research published in "The Black Family in Slavery and Freedom, 1750-1925" to test Moynihan's assumptions.[8]

Gutman's Findings:

- At the end of the Civil War, most families of formerly enslaved people had two parents present

- Many older couples had maintained long-term relationships despite slavery's disruptions

- Families showed remarkable resilience in creating new family bonds after being separated by sale

- African Americans demonstrated extraordinary adaptive capacity in maintaining family structures

Key Conclusion: Gutman concluded that Moynihan and Frazier had "underestimated the adaptive capacities of the enslaved and those born to them and their children."

Modern Implications:

This academic exchange highlights the importance of understanding both the real impacts of historical trauma AND the remarkable resilience that can also be inherited. Families carry both wounds and strengths from their past.

A.5: Practical Implications for Modern Families

What This Research Means:

1. **Validation:** Family patterns have real, biological foundations; they're not just "all in your head"

2. **Hope:** Just as negative patterns can be inherited, so can positive adaptations and resilience

3. **Awareness:** Understanding your family's history can help explain current challenges and strengths

4. **Intervention:** Conscious decisions and therapeutic work can interrupt negative cycles

5. **Legacy:** The choices you make today will influence not just your children but potentially your grandchildren

The Role of Choice:

While we inherit certain predispositions, research also indicates that conscious decision-making, therapy, spiritual practices, and environmental modifications can influence gene expression. By actively participating in these changes, we are not doomed to repeat our ancestors' patterns; we have the power to change our family's trajectory.

Breaking the Cycle:

Studies demonstrate that when one generation actively works to address inherited trauma and create positive changes, these improvements can also be passed down through epigenetic inheritance.[9] These studies provide scientific backing for the biblical principle that one person's choices can have a lasting impact on multiple generations.

A.6: Integration with Faith-Based Understanding

This scientific research doesn't contradict spiritual truth but rather provides additional evidence for what Scripture has long taught about generational patterns and the power of transformation. The same mechanisms that pass down negative patterns can also transmit:

- Resilience and strength

- Faith and spiritual practices

- Positive coping mechanisms

- Healthy relationship patterns

- Achievement motivation

Understanding both the scientific and spiritual dimensions provides a comprehensive view of how families can break destructive cycles and establish positive legacies for future generations.

Appendix A

For readers interested in exploring this research further, key studies can be found through PubMed and academic databases using search terms like "epigenetic inheritance," "intergenerational trauma," and "Holocaust survivor studies."[10]

Notes

Chapter 5: Understanding Brings Change

[1] For detailed information on family medical history and genetic predispositions, see resources from the Centers for Disease Control and Prevention (CDC) and National Institutes of Health (NIH).

Chapter 6: Tell the Story That Must Be Told

[2] Angelou, Maya. "On the Pulse of Morning," poem delivered at the inauguration of President Bill Clinton, January 20, 1993.

[3] Angelou, Maya. "Still I Rise," from *And Still I Rise: A Book of Poems* (New York: Random House, 1978).

Appendix A: The Science Behind Generational Inheritance

[4] Yehuda, Rachel, et al. "Holocaust Exposure Induced Intergenerational Effects on FKBP5 Methylation," *Biological Psychiatry* 80, no. 5 (2016): 372-380.

[5] Yehuda, Rachel, et al. "Influences of Maternal and Paternal PTSD on Epigenetic Regulation of the Glucocorticoid Receptor Gene in

Holocaust Survivor Offspring," *American Journal of Psychiatry* 171, no. 8 (2014): 872-879.

[6] Moynihan, Daniel Patrick. "The Negro Family: The Case for National Action," Office of Policy Planning and Research, U.S. Department of Labor, 1965.

[7] Frazier, E. Franklin. *The Negro Family in the United States* (Chicago: University of Chicago Press, 1939).

[8] Gutman, Herbert G. *The Black Family in Slavery and Freedom, 1750-1925* (New York: Pantheon Books, 1976).

[9] For current research on epigenetic inheritance, see publications from the National Institute of Mental Health and peer-reviewed journals such as *Nature, Science,* and *Cell.*

[10] Studies on intergenerational trauma transmission can be found through PubMed database using search terms: "epigenetic inheritance," "intergenerational trauma," and "transgenerational epigenetics."

Note: For readers interested in exploring the scientific research mentioned in this book, key studies can be accessed through academic databases such as PubMed (pubmed.ncbi.nlm.nih.gov) and Google Scholar (scholar.google.com).

About The Author

Tonia Leslie is the mother of five children who lives in the suburbs of Atlanta. She is a passionate author, speaker, minister and generational visionary who believes that legacy is the most sacred form of leadership. With deep roots in family, and faith, Tonia draws on personal experience to illuminate the beauty and complexity of working alongside those you love. Her writing blends real-life wisdom with practical strategy, offering a fresh, honest look at what it means to build something that lasts beyond a single lifetime.

Tonia brings clarity, grace, and grit to every conversation about inheritance, and identity. In this powerful debut, she shares the lessons, laughter, and losses that shaped her family's journey—and how purpose is the most valuable benefit of all.